The Best of Both Worlds

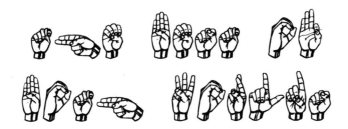

The Best of Both Worlds

(a-not-so-silent life)

Lila Worzel Miller

Writers Club Press
San Jose New York Lincoln Shanghai

The Best of Both Worlds
(a-not-so-silent life)

Writers Club Press
an imprint of iUniverse.com, Inc.

For information address:
iUniverse.com, Inc.
5220 S 16th, Ste. 200
Lincoln, NE 68512
www.iuniverse.com

ISBN: 0-595-14821-2

Printed in the United States of America

Dedicated to my parents
Miriam and Joseph Worzel

And for my children—
so they may always remember

Contents

Dedication v

Acknowledgements viii

Photographs ix

Chapter 1 Heritage 1

    Introduction 3

    Grandparents 5

    My Grandma and Grandpa 6

Chapter 2 Communication 13

    The Joy of Sign 17

    Signs 21

    Deaf and Dumb 26

    Deaf Shtick 27

Chapter 3 Parents 29

    Child Rearing 33

    Getting Away With Murder 36

    Dependency 38

    Grandma 42

    Mom 45

    The Ladies 52

    Daddy 55

    The Autobiography of Joe Worzel 58

    Renaissance Man 63

Chapter 4 Family and Friends 69

    Influences 71

George 72

Nancy 74

Ida and Bertye 77

Jerry 80

The Crowd 83

Uncle Joe 85

Chapter 5 Reminiscences 87

Nice Things 89

Sex 91

Romance 92

Courage 93

Need 94

Surprises 95

Mom's Diaries 97

Chapter 6 Memories 101

My Grandparents 103

Andy on Grandma 106

The Sounds of Silence 109

Chapter 7 Conclusions 111

Commentary 113

Memories 115

Recipes 117

Notes 119

About the Author 121

Acknowledgements

Grateful thanks to all my friends and family for their faithful support.

A special appreciation to my sons Howard and Andy for their input, to Mary Ann for getting me started, to Louise for helping me finish and especially to my husband, George for knowing when to leave and when to pitch in. Also for the schlepping up and down with the dictionaries and Thesaurus. More thanks to friend Gloria for listening and listening and listening....

Much appreciation to the tennis crowd, both here and in Florida. Marilyn S. for the many trips over and to the B.C. crowd for all those words.

Oscar, it was a good visit and helpful.

Stan—my computer maven—gratefulness forever for all the technical support and many, many lessons. I probably have been the dumbest student ever. Even so, I could never have finished without you.

Special thanks to Joe Desmond, Rabbi David, Bob Humber, Lew Goldwasser and all the residents of Tanya Towers. They enriched my mother's life when she most needed it—and mine.

Much appreciation to Joe Klempner and Avery Corman for their advice, wisdom and continuing support.

Marty Herlands, thanks for the pictures.

Of course, most thanks to my Mom and Dad for getting me here in the first place.

Photographs

1. Mom and Dad-Wedding picture
2. Manual Alphabet
3. Dad and Lila-Mom and Lila
4. Andy, Mom, Howard-Howard's Bar Mitzvah
   Howard, Mom, Andy-San Francisco
5. Mom-Lexington School
6. Sundays Ladies Lunch Club-
   Flo, Minnie, Frances, Lillian
   Mom, Bessie, Anna
7. Dad
8. Dad-Hall of Fame
9. Sisters-Mom, Ida and Bertye
10. Cousin Jerry
11. The Crowd-Dad, Flo, Harry, Mom
    Harry, Flo, Dad, Mom, Bessie, Moe, Gilbert
12. Mom and Dad

"We write to taste life twice;
in the moment and in retrospection."

Anais Nin

CHAPTER 1

Heritage

Introduction

An introduction to a book is like meeting people in the vestibule before showing them the apartment.

A childhood friend recently said, "Your parents were the happiest people I knew. I always loved coming to your house." She obviously got past the vestibule and into the apartment.

How then could I not share the silent beautiful language I learned to *speak* as the hearing child of deaf parents?

Another childhood friend, also with deaf parents, said, "I wouldn't change a minute of my childhood for anything in the world."

My childhood and formative years were shaped by happy, strong-willed parents and by the love and support given to me by relatives and the entire deaf community.

I am constantly reminded of how lucky I am to have been a part of two worlds. I wear my I LOVE YOU pendant with pride and it always brings a comment from people who haven't seen it before.

"How lovely!" How unusual!" "What does it mean?" "Oh really!" "How interesting!"

Have you ever seen deaf people signing (talking) to each other? It is expressive, graceful, beautiful and quite revealing.

Were my parents handicapped? They didn't think so. Deaf people do most everything hearing people do. They drive cars, work in every field, play sports and even become President of a college. (Gallaudet University in Washington D.C.)

Was I handicapped, deprived of my childhood, forced to take care of my parents? NOT SO! I had THE BEST OF BOTH WORLDS!

Let's not forget there are advantages also to being deaf. One activity I fear most is going to the dentist. Why? It's really not pain but the sound of the drill. Not a problem for deaf people. Then there's the time the call came that my Dad had passed away. We were downstairs and Mom was upstairs sewing. We had time to compose ourselves before telling Mom.

I have always worked best under stress, whether cramming for an exam, packing for a trip or planning a party. Perhaps this is why it has taken me so long to finish this writing. Perhaps not. I rather think it was a reluctance to let go and when finally finished, what then, or as Mom said, "Where to next?" I celebrate their lives with this memoir. The words may be short but the memories are forever.

Journey with me into the joy of sign language. Some of these stories may be apocryphal handed down over time, repeated over and over to me and my children, but they remain gifts of my childhood. I promise you laughter, tears and a learning experience.

Grandparents

I start my stories with my children's thoughts on their grandparents. I include an essay written by my son Howard, shortly before Mom's passing and one by my other son Andy, who delivered the eulogy at Mom's funeral. They express themselves as grandchildren who had the benefit and good fortune of having had loving grandparents.

I begin and end with these and space the others as bookmarks along life's way.

My Grandma and Grandpa

My Grandparents traveled the world. Once my Grandmother told me they visited Amsterdam.

"Really?" I asked. I had been to Amsterdam.

"Yes," answered Grandma. "Amsterdam. Beautiful city, very pretty." Grandma stroked her face, using the sign for "pretty."

"Did you visit the red light district?" I asked. I always attempted to test Grandma's limits.

Grandma smiled. "Yes, yes, we saw it. The men all went at night. I told your grandfather go ahead, go on if you like."

My eyes widened. Grandma nodded her head.

"Did he go?" I whispered.

Grandma smiled, and shook her head, imitating all too well my Grandfather's expression, the one he used for "No thank you."

I first ate ice cream with my Grandpa. I was two, maybe three years old. He was wheeling me down the street in my baby carriage.

Grandpa bought some ice cream, a small scoop in a cup. Vanilla. Offered me a bite. I shook my head. Didn't want any.

He offered me again. A small sample, a bit of vanilla on one of those wooden spoons. Pushed the spoon toward my lips. I pulled back my head.

Grandpa recounted this story to me when I was eight or nine. Grandpa loved to tell stories, his expressions and movements full of life. Punctuated his tales with sounds and grunts, noises only a deaf person can make. To those who have never heard these sounds, they are often frightening. To me they were simply Grandpa.

He told the ice cream story in this fashion. Mimicked baby Andy pulling his head from the wooden spoon. But Grandpa was persistent, finally touching the ice cream to my lips. Baby Andy pulled his head again, his face recoiling in horror. But then a transformation occurred.

The moment the ice cream touched my lips the grimace disappeared. The eyes widened. A smile formed.

Grandpa acted the transformation. He pulled back the spoon, and suddenly it was baby Andy coming forward. Baby Andy wanting another taste. Grandpa would smile, proud of this moment.

Of course he offered the rest of the ice cream. Grandpa could never refuse anything I wanted. And thus I enjoyed ice cream for the first time. Vanilla. To this day my favorite flavor.

My grandparents had a one bedroom apartment blocks away from ours in the Bronx. Visiting my grandparents was always a treat.

My parents would be in the living room, the television might be on. My grandfather would appear in the hallway, would catch my attention. He'd motion to me, his thumb in front of his lips. Sign language for *secret*. Then he'd move his hand, pressing his thumb and forefinger against his cheek, turning his hand in a forward motion. *Chewing gum.*

I'd sneak out of my chair, into the hallway, where Grandpa would slip a two-pack of Chiclets into my hand. Yes, it was always a treat to visit my grandparents.

P.S. My first trip to the dentist revealed 18 cavities. Mom no longer thought our secret was cute. But the trick continued. Chiclets, however, was replaced with Trident.

It was second grade. Mom was working, so I would walk to my grandparents' apartment in the Bronx for lunch. Imagine, a second grader walking alone in the Bronx. But it happened.

This particular time, crisis intervened. I had split my pants in school, right down the rear. Total embarrassment. The lunch bell rang and I flew out, practically running to my grandparents. I didn't know what they could do, but I was determined I would not go back to school with ripped pants. No way.

Not to worry. Grandma served my lunch, a meatloaf sandwich, and while I ate she sewed. My pants were mended, I was fed, and I went back to school. Grandma always made things right.

I was in fourth grade. My family had just moved out of the Bronx, to our new house in Rockland County. Suburbia. A new place. New kids. New rules.

It was frightening to fit in. Boys being boys meant plenty of fights. Lots of competition.

One day the kids were playing Kickball in the circle. Kickball is played like baseball, only with a large red ball, that you kicked.

I was watching. Hadn't been invited to play, and in a way, I was glad. I wasn't sure if I'd be good enough.

The kids were playing, and there was a close play at third. An argument: safe or out? Grandpa was with me, visiting the new home for the first (and as it turned out, the last) time.

The argument grew heated as crucial plays in kickball often did. Safe! Out! Safe! Suddenly Grandpa leapt on the scene, his arms sweeping across in the "safe!" motion. Again, and again, a confident, umpire-like move. "Safe!" One of the boys in the argument pointed to Grandpa, the others looked. "Safe!"

I felt a moment of fear. Had Grandpa overstepped his boundary? We were, after all, the new ones on the block.

But the boys stopped arguing. Grandpa's "safe!" stood. Everybody agreed, and went back to playing.

Grandpa walked away. Smiled at me. After that I was always welcomed to play.

I was visiting Grandma once when I was in college. She was alone then, my grandfather having passed away.

I told her about my new girlfriend, the first "serious" one I ever had. Grandma listened enthusiastically. But then she surprised me.

"Be careful," she warned. "Girls will get pregnant, and then you're caught."

Talk about generation gap. The possibility that a girl, never mind one who loved me, would purposely get pregnant, well, it was beyond my comprehension. But even if it was…

"So?" I asked. "If she gets pregnant, I don't have to marry her."

It was Grandma's turn to be surprised. But then she smiled. "New times," she said. "But still, be careful."

Grandpa always carried a small notebook in his breast pocket. An old leather notebook, the cover practically falling off. Also carried a pencil.

"Always," he signed to me, his expression communicating the seriousness of this habit. "My best friend," he signed.

Grandpa explained that whenever he got in a situation where someone didn't understand him, he'd write it on paper. Problem solved.

"My best friend," he said again, and I understood what he meant.

My Grandfather, Joseph Worzel, once caught three foul balls at a Major League Baseball game. In *one* inning. Three foul balls. Grandpa told me this fact on several occasions, always rightfully proud. Three foul balls.

The years passed, my Grandfather died, but stories about his legend grew. Beyond legend, however, was character. The one thing everyone agreed about my Grandfather—he was a man of his word. Told stores, sure, but never made them up.

Three foul balls. In one inning. As far as I know, a Major League record.

Grandma came home late one night, when my mother was a child, maybe eight or nine. Mom was sleeping and Grandma tucked her in. That's when Grandma noticed that Mom was chewing gum. In her sleep.

Well Grandma was worried she might choke, so proceeded to remove the gum in mid chew—while Mom was still asleep. I can still see Grandma demonstrating how she pulled out the gum.

The next day Grandma asked Mom where she got the gum. Where did she get a penny? Mom had to come clean. "I took it," she explained.

Grandma marched Mom down to the store and forced her to confess to the owner. Mom was in tears as she handed a penny to the sympathetic man. And once again, Grandma had set things right.

Grandma visited once when we had moved upstate. Our parents were away, and my brother had just learned to drive. The question was where to go for dinner.

We narrowed it down to two choices, Chinese vs. Italian. We decided to let Grandma choose.

"Eenie meanie minie mo, catch a nigger by the toe…"

My jaw dropped. So did my brother's. Grandma didn't understand what was wrong.

"That's a bad word, Grandma," I explained. "Very bad."

She was surprised. The expression didn't mean anything to her good or bad, was just a way to choose. My brother explained that now we said, "…catch a *tiger* by the toe."

Grandma learned, and always used "tiger" from then on. And my brother and I, our lesson was that one is never to old to learn.

Up to fourth grade my family lived in an apartment in the Bronx, on the ninth floor. Mom was teaching those days, and often my Grandfather would baby-sit for my brother and myself. Grandpa was always fun to have baby-sit.

Every afternoon the Good Humor truck would come. Ring its famous bell. And kids would gather, buying ice cream, candy, soda...

We'd be upstairs, would hear the bell, run out to the terrace. Nine stories below was the Good Humor truck. Ringing its bell.

We'd tell Grandpa, terribly excited and all. Afraid we'd miss the truck, miss our chance for ice cream.

But Grandpa was cool. Always cool. Calm. He'd gather his stuff, walk with out the apartment. Down the hall. Down the elevator, through the lobby, out the back, past the playground...to the parking lot. The Good Humor truck.

And we never missed it. Never.

I remember my grandparents. I remember the last time I saw my Grandfather. My parents and brother went to a Broadway show, and I went to their apartment. That was more fun to me than any show.

Nothing special happened; cards with my Grandfather, a ballgame on TV, a good meal. My Grandfather reprimanded me in fact, asked how come I wasn't better behaved like my brother. But he said it with love.

My grandparents were full of love, full of life. I remember their friends gathered in their apartment, the back and forth dialogue of deaf people debating, arguing, yelling. The sounds, the grunts, the expressions.

I remember my grandparents sliding smoothly from the deaf world to the hearing. Never once thinking they were "handicapped." To this day when a friend tells me they "spoke" to their grandparents, well it's strange to me. Having grandparents who were deaf was my norm. And my privilege.

I remember my Grandmother's smile. I remember her holding me, hugging me, telling me to "be brave" the night my Grandfather died. I remember the way my Grandfather always carried himself. My grandparents taught by example. To live, to love, and to let others live and love.

My Grandparents were for me, the best of both worlds.

CHAPTER 2

Communication

"The inability to hear is a nuisance;
the inability to communicate is the tragedy."

Lou Ann Walker

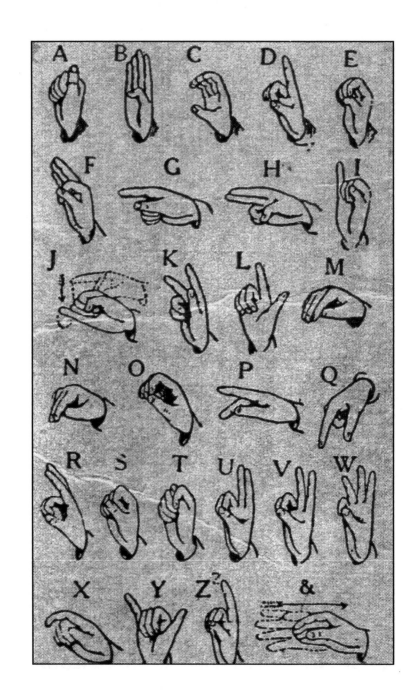

The Joy of Sign

My Mother is gone for several years and I find myself inexplicably drawn to old ties.

I've visited her last residence in New York to see some of the old gang, to talk with them, people I didn't really know so well in my youth but grew close to when Mom moved downtown.

There is an intimacy, beauty, and comfort in signing that is hard to explain. Nuances such as stuttering, shouting, murmurs, (usually vocal), can indeed be conveyed in sign (often accompanied by high-pitched tones.) Deaf people are not silent.

My parents would sometimes interpret for me and I for them. They helped bridge my world with the silent world—my mainland and their island. It was as if I belonged to an exclusive club. I was bilingual before the term became popular.

Sign is a strong bond. If a deaf person travels from one city to another and meets another person using sign, it's as if they found a long lost friend.

Perhaps it is the same when a newcomer to this country comes from work or school and goes home to their family and feels the comfort of their native language. Just like when we, the hearing, visit another country and feel somewhat limited when we shop or deal with a merchant. If someone steps in and says, "May I help you, I speak English?" a smile comes to our faces. It is the familiarity and closeness that makes us feel good.

Thus it is the signing that I miss, that draws me back over and over again to the comfort of yesteryear.

I grew up as a fun-loving child, knowing that my parents were in charge. I turned to them for advice, love, support and always received it.

Yes I knew sign language, but my parents exposed me to the outside world even before entering school. They made sure I had a radio, used the telephone, and encouraged outside friendships.

There is a current trend for the young deaf in many parts of the country to use only oral communication. To exclude signing cuts off a means of communication between two deaf people, much like not allowing hearing people to have speech. Imagine not being able to share secrets, thoughts or confidences with all the nuances that come with sign or speech?

I believe people with hearing loss should live well, equally in both worlds, hearing and deaf, therefore all means of communication are necessary.

Ask any immigrant to this country. They quickly learn English, but never forget their native language.

Hearing parents of deaf children need both means of communication, oral and sign. Their children should have the same.

I recently saw a movie about a hearing couple with a deaf child, (Mr. Holland's Opus.) They had been told to have only oral communication with their child.

The child was almost two years old and still grunting and crying in frustration at trying to be understood. The mother then burst out crying, screaming to her husband, "I want to TALK to my child! I NEED to communicate with him. I NEED him to know how much I love him. There must be a way!"

Well, of course there is. There always is. Why speak only English if you are fluent in two languages?

For children there usually isn't a problem. They learn more easily and quickly than their parents. The hearing parents of deaf children are the ones who have to adapt and learn sign along with their children. They should use sign AND voice to communicate with each other and share their feelings and thoughts. After all, when we are in school, we learn another language. So why not SIGN?

"Deaf children work hard to acquire and learn the same things that children with ALL their senses do. Let's not make it more difficult."

Helen Keller

"The Living Word Awakened my soul,
gave it light, hope, joy, set it free."

Helen Keller

Signs

People ask, "Was it difficult for you growing up with deaf parents? How did you learn how to speak?" There seems to be a general assumption that if one is deaf or handicapped in any way, —ergo, one must be uneducated or stupid.

There was always a radio in the house and my folks made sure I was exposed to everything the outside world had to offer. I was taken to ballet and tap dancing class, (because that's what little girls did) and even to acting class, for I was a natural mime, as are many hearing children of deaf parents. Sign language, with all its grace and gestures, naturally leads to acting and mimicking.

When I was growing up, I mostly used Signed English along with the American Sign Language (ASL) that is accepted today in many colleges and universities. Signed English uses each word in a sentence while ASL is an abbreviated sentence structure. I think Signed English sometimes has an advantage when it comes to beauty. For instance the first words I ever "spoke" were signed, "I love you."

"I"—the manual alphabet "I" (pinky finger up).

"Love"—two arms crossed in front of the chest (as if in a hug).

"You"—your pointer finger pointed at the person you are talking to.

All together signed.

"I love you," as three separate words seems much more expressive than the current symbol universally used such as my pendant. Try it and see. As a universal sign and a quicker way, the symbol is a nice gesture. But signing "I-Love-You" has so much more meaning to me.

After "I-Love-You" usually before a year (for my son and myself it was 7 months of age) came "I Love You With All My Heart."

"With"—your two fists together.

"All"—your two hands winding around each other.

"My"—your open hand put on your chest.

"Heart"—your middle finger pointed at your heart.

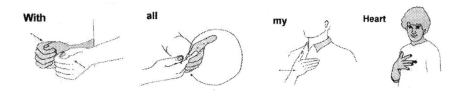

With   all   my   Heart

All together it flows gracefully.

Signs were a great help when I was in public school. All my friends knew how to sign numbers, which in sign language is done on one hand instead of two. Some also knew the alphabet. (I'm sure you can see the advantages of that during test-taking.) Sign also came in handy playing the game "Signals" as a teenager, not to mention that all important college activity "Charades."

People have a nasty tendency to whisper or talk behind one's back, be it a deaf person a blind person or even a person of a different nationality. Well, the tables can certainly be turned. My folks and I could always "talk" about someone or "whisper" behind *their* back.

Often on the subway train, Mom, Dad and I would sit next to each other and begin to talk rapidly in sign, not mouthing a word. This was done purposely to attract attention and it always worked, people being people. Soon passengers would grin to each other, giggle and go,

"Tch-tch." (Remember, this was in the 30's and 40's.) After completing the entrapment, I would look up at a passenger and as loud as I could, say, "What time is it please?" or "How many stops to 42nd street?"

The shocked look on their faces would crack us up and we would nudge each other gleefully. Oh what devils we thought we were!

In emergency situations *Sign* comes in handy. Once, when I was seven or so, my Mom and I were taking the subway downtown. The train was crowded. We came to our stop and my Mom managed to squeeze out whereas I was pushed and jostled and, oh my, the doors closed and there we were, Mom on the platform and me on the train, which started to move.

"Get off at the next station!" Mom commanded, in *Sign*. "Wait for me. I'll take the next train. Don't worry, I'll be there shortly. STAY!"

I did. She came. Whew!

Another time we both got off the train, but as the doors closed we realized we left a suitcase on the floor right where we were sitting. We signaled to a passenger to open the window and pass the suitcase through the window. He very kindly did, so you see some signs are universal.

In the hearing world, people have nicknames: Spike, Babe, Lefty. In the deaf world most people have their own *special* sign. My Dad, Joe was expressed by putting your pointer finger behind one ear and rotating the finger. This was due to the small holes behind each lobe from mastoid operations he had as a child. My Mom Miriam was a chubby teen-ager, so her name was formed by signIng the letter "M" and lightly patting one's cheek to signify her chubby cheeks.

Their friend Moe used to have a mustache. His name was signed by placing the second finger under the nose. That was his sign—even after the mustache was gone.

My name was simply the letter "L" waved back and forth.

Some people had their names spelled out just for the beauty of the spelling done fluidly in one sweeping movement. I miss this so much.

Avery Corman, author of Kramer vs. Kramer whose aunt and uncle were deaf, said, "A major part of my life, my childhood, was illuminated by the language described here."

"Silence is as eloquent as words."

Jose Quintero

Deaf and Dumb

Some people say hearing music plays on one's emotions. Sometimes silence is golden. The last ten minutes of a recent movie (Big Night) ended with no talking. No words were needed to convey the emotion and gist of the scene.

Back in the 1920's and 1930's it was common to refer to deaf people as deaf and dumb.

Dumb was a euphemism meaning without speech, but to the world at large the term meant, literally, dumb-stupid.

Even when my father played basketball in an industrial league with hearing persons, he was referred to as Dummy. This practice was accepted by deaf people. (Today most deaf people would respond, "Please, DEAF only, not dumb, if you don't mind.")

My "Aunt" Minnie, (Mom's dearest and oldest friend) told me how she met my mother, her first deaf friend. (Minnie herself was hard of hearing and had a deaf child.) A neighbor told her, "There's a nice deaf and dumb woman downstairs. "Minnie answered, "Don't say dumb, just say deaf."

This was 1932. Minnie always was the modern woman.

Deaf and dumb-how archaic! To me it is so funny, particularly for my parents. Joe worked thirty years as a linotype operator for the NEW YORK POST, was President of the Hebrew Association of the Deaf (H.A.D.) and a member of the National Hall of Fame of the Deaf for Basketball. Miriam was a dressmaker par excellence for fancy boutiques, card shark and general bon vivant.

Today, the accepted term is deaf or hearing-loss. Progress-we hope.

Deaf Shtick

There are certain gimmicks, quirks that belong solely to the deaf culture.

1) If you enter a room and deaf people have their backs to you and you want their attention, flip the light switch on and off a few times.

2) Card playing. There is a reason for the universal appeal of cards to the deaf culture. One does not have to hear to play. In fact it was my sons who pointed out that being deaf is probably an asset in cards, eliminating outside noises and helping to concentrate and focus. They told me, "Grandpa taught us how to play cards. That's why we're such good players." "I don't understand," I said. "He taught us how to concentrate and count."

Both sons seem to have inherited their grandparents' card-playing skills. As soon as possible, they started playing together—Crazy 8's, Poker, Casino, Rummy. Later on all of us would spend an evening playing cards.

Every evening before dinner, I would play pinochle with my father until my mom would come in from the kitchen and wave, "Come in." Dad would invariably signal, "One more minute," which would always lead to mom coming in again and the familiar hands on waist stance signifying, "WELL?"

3) A deaf signal for the last card or last hand is a KNOCK on the table.

4) There is a hearing yell and then there's a deaf yell and believe me you will listen to a DEAF YELL (A high-pitched or guttural shrill).

5) Whistling. My father could put his two fingers in his mouth and give a really loud signal. We lived on the 4th floor of an apartment building and I could always hear when my Dad was calling. I would

stick my head out of the window and he would sign to me what he wanted, usually, "Should I go get some ice-cream?" Now I don't really know if this applied to all deaf people, but that was a special signal between my Dad and me.

There are so many logical yet, special nuances associated with the deaf world which only helps to make that world more special.

CHAPTER 3

Parents

picture—three of us

Child Rearing

How do deaf (handicapped) people tend to babies and raise their children? Is it possible? Well, of course it's possible!

"The difference between the possible and the impossible—the impossible takes a little longer."

David Ben Gurion

During infancy my deaf parents tied a string from their finger to the crib so they could feel any movement. How did they ever get any sleep? I don't know! How did I learn to speak? By being surrounded with hearing people, friends, relatives, radios—all talking to me. But mostly being hugged and loved.

I signed, "I love you" before speaking. For that matter so did my sons, because we learned that from mom and dad, grandma and grandpa. I also knew every nursery rhyme as mom made sure to tell and retell them all to me. My sister-in-law once said, "All babies need for the first six months is a lot of loving and hugging." How true!

My husband and I knew our older son had an almost perfect ear for music when at two years of age, he sang, "Rain rain go away"—completely off key. Then we realized he was imitating his grandmother, *perfectly*, off key.

Contrary to the popular belief that hearing children of deaf parents are overindulged and spoiled, independence and responsibility were impressed upon us consistently.

I once came home chewing gum. Mom knew I didn't have any money. "Where did you get the gum?" I shrugged. Mom knew me better. I finally admitted that I took a penny from the newsstand outside the candy store, and went in and bought the gum. Well, she promptly took me right back to the store and made me return the penny. EMBARRASS-ING! But I learned my lesson. So much for being overindulged!

Once in high school I hurt my foot in gym. Mom was called (through a neighbor) to come and get me. Well it involved two buses, but she got there. We were on the bus going home and passed one of her favorite shopping areas. I guess I was obviously all right as she said, "You go right home, I'll just get a few things." Some babying! (Deep down I knew she was a wreck by the way she came huffing and puffing into the infirmary. She just always held her emotions in check.) At the same time she held me responsible for myself.

During my early years, Mom sewed most of my clothes, even coats. If I needed a blouse for the next day, it was sewn that night. Of course, not to "spoil" me, if one was available, it was my responsibility to iron it. I hate ironing to this day. Later as adults, shopping for clothes became a mother-daughter ritual and a fun kind of outing. We would go to the stores and try on hats just for fun and giggle. We would go to a fancy apartment house off Central Park and make believe we were apartment hunting-again, just for fun.

If I wanted to go to the neighborhood movie on Saturdays with my friends it was my job to take the empty bottles to the store and get the deposit money to pay for the movie.

As far as dependability and trust, there are certain responsibilities in life that parents, deaf or hearing just do. No such questions like, "Is it convenient? Am I tired?" An emergency calls for reflex action. This is all part of child rearing.

I never felt any sense of fear because my parents were deaf. Their other senses were exceptionally heightened. Once Mom and I were visiting her friend. She had a young daughter who locked me in the bathroom. We were both about eight or nine but she was bigger than I. I couldn't get past her to get out. I yelled and pounded at the door over and over. Mom sensed my absence and came to the door. She realized I couldn't get out and called the Superintendent. Fortunately the apartment wasn't too high up. He got a ladder and opened the bathroom window, came in and opened the door. I realized only about twenty years ago that this might be a reason for my being somewhat claustraphobic. I don't much like tunnels and I do leave the bathroom door slightly ajar in my own house.

My husband and I had a car accident in Florida shortly after we were married, and were hospitalized. I don't know how she did it, but there was Mom the next day. Somehow she got to the plane all by herself and taxied to the hospital to be with us. This was all part of motherhood.

When our younger son had an emergency appendectomy, I just sat in the waiting room and cried for hours at the helplessness of the situation. The next day, there was Dad, before I even arrived, comparing scars with his grandson. He waited for no one to take him anywhere.

When my Dad had carotid artery surgery (I was the one who sent him to the doctor in the first place) I threw up, cried, and was a wreck waiting while my Mom said, "He'll be fine." He was.

When I returned to work after my sons were in school, it was grandma and grandpa who gave them lunch every day. They had sandwiches, "cut in three sections," the boys told all their friends. Grandpa waited on the school corner to make sure of the safety of his grandsons crossing the street.

All in all it was a mutual give and take, but I think I got the better of the deal. As for growing up with deaf parents, they made my life a song.

Getting Away With Murder

I was by no means a goody-goody. Having deaf parents certainly did have its advantages. Telling secrets and gossiping on the telephone was one of them. Another was later on when dates would bring me home at night. I think that needs no explanation.

Once we were visiting friends upstate. The crowd was sitting and gabbing in the sun-room and I decided to take advantage by taking my friend's bike out of the garage to learn how to ride. The fact that there was a gravel driveway and a steep incline didn't stop me. Off I went pedaling along and CRASH! Down I went onto the gravel, skinning my knee. These friends had a dog that had been keeping me company and he proceeded to bark and bark and bark. I kept saying shh not wanting to incur the wrath of my parents as well as our hosts. Even though they couldn't hear, deaf people are very in tune with movement. I managed to keep the dog still and get the bike back and, yes, I got away with it—that time.

In school I was known as a chatterbox. In fact, in the sixth grade when we had sewing, the teacher gave me a model of a bird called The Red Chatterer. I think that fit me pretty much to a T.

Each term would bring a new teacher to break in which ultimately would lead to "I WANT TO SEE YOUR MOTHER!"

In trudged Mom, not happy but doing her motherly duty. Now my Mom could speak quite well, not having been born deaf, but of course had trouble hearing. She would have the usual pat answer ready. "Lila's very high strung."

I never did find out the exact meaning of high strung, but it got me off the hook each time. My teachers probably decided I didn't have much opportunity to talk at home. What a joke! I'll explain later.

When I was in the eighth grade I had my first male teacher and instantly developed a crush. Open School Week came and I asked my mom to come to school. "Are you crazy? The first time a teacher hasn't sent for me and you want me to come?"

The absolute best was when the teachers would say, "I want to see your FATHER!"

Little did they know that he was an absolute pussycat. In he came, pad and pencil in hand. (I never told my teachers my parents were deaf—they wouldn't believe me anyway.) Besides, there was nothing his daughter could do wrong. (At that time in my life, according to my mother, EVERYTHING I did was wrong.) Later on in years, she did a complete reversal and I became her darling daughter.

Anyway, after a few minutes with Daddy and his charming ways the teachers were always swayed and I got through another term.

So you see, there are advantages to having,

THE BEST OF BOTH WORLDS.

Dependency

Dependent? BULLSHIT!! My parents were fiercely and proudly independent. I am tired of reading about all these gripes and pet peeves of hearing children regarding their deaf parents.

"Oh the guilt trips they put on us!" Such long-suffering angst of these martyrs!

We were a special group—children of deaf parents—growing up in a unique place and time. Depression, post-depression (Was there really a depression? I never knew it), World War 11. Was that special breed of parenting the last to instill a sense of love, community, sharing and most of all, education? I hope not. Education and communication were top priorities.

Someone else order in a restaurant for my Dad? Never! My father always carried pen and paper in every pocket of every jacket or coat. When the waiter would come over my father would simply give him the order on paper.

A friend of mine whose parents were good friends of my folks recently shared this story with me: When she was about nine years old, her Mom asked her to call an insurance agent for her. She did, and then the agent asked her various questions to which my friend, being the dutiful daughter, began to reply.

"What are you doing?" her Mom asked. "He was asking me some questions," she replied. "Hang right up! Get this straight. The only thing I can't do for myself is call someone on the phone. (This is years before the existence of the Teletypewriter-phone (TTY) for the hearing impaired.)

If there are questions to answer, you ask me. I am your MOTHER, and if you can't get that through your head then I'll just have to go down to the office and take care of it myself."

When I was married my husband and I would often take drives with my folks. Before we even started my father would have all the bridge tolls out and ready and believe me there was no arguing with him as to who would pay. If an argument would start, my father would close his eyes and smile.

We never went hungry. There was always plenty of food and good times. One of the best parts of growing up was those special Saturday evenings when the crowd (five couples I'll talk about later) would come over. Cards and eating! OOH! Those goodies! Nuts and raisins mixed, apricots and marshmallows put together like an Oreo cookie. (Does anyone still do that anymore?) And the best part was the next day—all those leftovers. Mom's specialty was chocolate mousse pie.

I remember picnics—games—outings. Deaf parents with mostly hearing children, some deaf. It didn't matter, bilingual, you see.

Life was never dull. School during the week (the hearing world) and get togethers on weekends. THE BEST OF BOTH WORLDS.

Dependent parents were certainly not the case in my family or anyone else in the crowd.

Grandma

by Howard Miller

There is an elderly woman I know, who sits many miles away from me. She is now frail, and her mind isn't always functioning with the rest of the world. Her eyes only too briefly, show a trace of her past sparkle and her body has betrayed the years of her beauty and her pride in taking care of herself.

This woman is my Grandma. But when I think of my Grandma, I see back into what my Grandma was. I see a woman who loved her family but also had a large circle of friends. I see a woman who my friends liked because she was fun to be with, pleasant to be around. I see a woman who didn't judge, didn't complain, didn't criticize. I see a woman who taught me politeness, independence and how physical limitations shouldn't limit your life.

I see a woman who I played cards with, who I went bowling with, who told the longest stories that went absolutely nowhere, and who I told things to that I wouldn't tell my parents, knowing she wouldn't tell them either.

This is the woman I see when I look at my Grandma. And if I ever get discouraged looking at my Grandma these days, I only need look at my Mother, for in her eyes, I see my beautiful and wonderful Grandma.

"God Couldn't Be Everywhere
So He Created Mothers."

Hebrew Proverb

Mom

Mothers are special people we have been told, and being one myself, who am I to argue?

My mother was a brave soul, taking life as it came. She was stoical in her outlook and calmly faced the world. There are many instances when she helped to allay my fears by objectively explaining the facts.

Mom was extremely protective. One day I was in my ninth month of pregnancy. My folks, husband and I were out in a park. A dog suddenly came bounding towards us. I might add, at that time, mom was afraid of dogs, but nevertheless stood in front of me, her arms opened wide for my protection. Fortunately, the dog was just playful.

Once my family (the four of us) and mom were driving over a bridge. Our car went into a spin. Round and round until it came to a CRASH at the divider. My husband and I were in front and mom was in back between the two boys. All I could think of as the car was turning was to stay awake and to yell to the kids to keep their heads down but I couldn't utter a word. Not to worry. When we finally stopped, I looked around and there was mom, an arm around each boy, all huddled together and heads down.

Mom was afraid of dogs but our dog Cricket, was different. Not just a pet but a member of the family (What dog isn't?). Cricket knew mom couldn't hear. Really! When she wanted her attention, instead of barking, she would go to mom and put her paws on her and mom knew that meant Cricket wanted to cuddle in her lap.

My dad died two days before my older son's Bar Mitzvah and it was mom's urging to go on with the celebration. "Life goes on."

Dad had been practicing vocalizing the Hebrew prayers over and over again. He was to be called up to the *bimah* to receive an honor as was customary for parents and grandparents. This was to be a big moment as it is for any parent or Grandpa. I was at their apartment one day and the next day got the call from mom who simply said, "I think Daddy had a stroke. Come."

She managed to call my husband at work and got someone to call an ambulance. Dad suffered a stroke. At first we thought it might just be minor but it turned out to be a cerebral hemorrhage. Dad lapsed into a coma for nine days. Mom and I and, of course George came to the hospital. Within one day all of mom's friends were there. It was highly emotional watching dad and thinking about the big event the following week. Mom cried, something I rarely saw, but kept her spirits up bolstered by her friends. We all believed dad would pull through as no one expects her Father to die-ever.

When the call finally came, one night, mom was at our house altering her dress for the Bar-Mitzvah. After some biting of the lip and a cry, she went in to comfort Andy, our younger son. And Mom made the decision to go on with the celebration as she didn't want Howard to remember all his life having it cancelled. Brave lady!

She was by no means all peaches and cream. She was very strong willed, and as she called me high strung, I would have to say she was headstrong. Before the advent of the TTY, she would call me on the phone (she was hard of hearing) ask me a few questions, then say, "I can't understand. Just come see me tomorrow." And that would be that.

Guilt! Don't ask! Guilt is not only the province of the hearing world. Mom had a cousin who would occasionlly visit. He signed beautifully, and boy did she let me know it. "Better than you!" she would sign.

I did, however, finally get my due. In later years, when Mom moved downtown to a residence for the deaf, I began to sign with many of the neighbors. One day, right in front of Mom, one of her friends said, "You sign just like a deaf person." The ultimate compliment! I looked at my Mother, grinned and made a face that said, "So there!!"

We had cousins who were very good to Mom and who lived downtown. They would often take her to dinner and to the ballet. Mom, being independent, would go downtown by subway, but then, I would hear, "Kathy and Alan put me into a taxi to go home, and gave me $20 for the cab. So there!!" (As if to show off or put some guilt on me.)

"Terrific," I would answer, and we'd both laugh.

Is it a universal motherly shtick, this waving good-bye until you're out of sight thing? I would visit Mom and when leaving for the elevator, she would stand at the door, and both of us would continually wave till the elevator came and I entered.

I find that I do the same thing with my own sons, be it leaving the house by car, or boarding a plane.

Mom had a generous and kind heart. After meeting my future mother-in-law, Mom told me, "She's very nice! Now you be good to her."

Mom once wanted to visit an elderly woman who was living in a deaf residence near where my family lived. Mom asked me to take her to see this woman, "If you don't mind." (Her favorite expression.)

It was a beautiful and emotional visit, for me anyway. Two people who hadn't seen each other for twenty years or so suddenly meeting. I saw mom give the lady a twenty dollar bill and felt like I had done a good deed.

Mom loved the smell of the fireplace logs burning and smiled when she heard the crackle. She would always ask us to light the fire when she came to visit.

Mom could take the most mundane experiences and turn them into something quite comical. Visualize this setting:

The office of one of New York's most prominent ophthalmologists, filled to capacity with waiting patients. Mom and I were sitting, talking, reading for quite some time. Mom had decided she was not going to have her cataract removed the old fashioned way. No long stay in a hospital for her. She had read about the new laser way of cataract removal, and this famous doctor. So here we were, waiting and waiting. I really don't remember the fee, except that it was certainly more than any other doctor—say, $200. Mom took the scene in quietly, looked at me and signed, "$200, $200, $200, $200," going around the room pointing to each person as she signed, "$200." I broke up, laughing. The visit lasted about ten minutes, so at $200 each, Mom's point seemed to be right on target. I might add that Mom did have her cataract removed by this man and it turned out successfully—SO THERE! (Another of mom's expressions and right on target when proved right.)

Once, Mom came for a visit and we went with a friend of mine to the local high school for an exercise class. We were seated on the gym floor, one next to each other. The instructor asked us to count off, which of course Mom didn't hear. It started with the first lady, "ONE-TWO-THREE-FOUR," I said, turning and poking Mom at the same time. Well, she gave me such a look and POKED ME RIGHT BACK, saying, "FOUR." The whole class had a laugh and so did Mom when I explained. Then it was a clear, loud, "FIVE!" and she turned to the next person in line.

Recently while at a Spa, a smile came over me picturing Mom looking around (sometimes we would indulge ourselves and get a facial or massage together) pointing to each amenity and saying, "FANCY". She would draw out the word both in speech and sign.

Our family had the good fortune to go on vacation together in 1986. It was always Mom's dream to go to Hawaii.

My husband and I decided it would be okay to take her along, so we made plans. Our older son was working in San Francisco and decided Grandma needed a roommate, and at the same time our younger son had just graduated from college and was off to Los Angeles.

So there we were, five of us, off to Hawaii, or as Mom loved to say, "The whole family."

Mom insisted on paying her share. Our older son devised a plan to make paying for dining out easier and less complicated. Daddy would pay for dinner the first day, older son would pay day two, Grandma day three, and younger son, not yet employed, was our graduation treat. Somehow, the bills for days one and two were always twice as much as Grandma's day. After a couple of times, she said, "How come my turn is so much less?"

Finally catching on, she said, "My turn today. I want a fancy place, if you don't mind."

Well, we tried, didn't we?

"Here's To The Ladies Who Lunch!"

Steven Sondheim

The Ladies

The ladies were a remarkable group of women. It always amazed me that they met somewhere at the right time and right place without having their own phones.

Mom would ask a neighbor to call my "aunt " Minnie's neighbor with a message and somehow the arrangements were circulated. Mom's closest friends, Minnie, Bessie and Flo, always. Then sometimes, Frances, Anna and Lillian, all pictured on the previous page. Hilda and Bernie were usually met together. Bernie was actually under Mom's care when mom was a supervisor at the Lexington School for the Deaf. They were a little younger and remained loyal friends to Mom way after Dad's passing, visiting Mom after she broke her hip and continued to do so when Mom eventually moved downtown.

The calls would be made and off Mom would go, walk to the subway, up the stairs on her way downtown and there they would all be at the right time and right restaurant. Mom was known for being, "a little late" so if they were to meet at 1p.m. Mom would be told 12:45. Somehow, after I was married Mom was never late. My husband, George could never understand how anyone could think Mom was late. Who knows, maybe it was his influence. He likes to think so.

The Ladies would meet at a favorite restaurant, gab go over the week's events, then on to The Club for some cards. The important thing was to get a "good" table. After playing they would then go out for some dinner. If it was a weekend, Mom might sleep over at Minnie's house. She'll explain more about that later on in her "Diaries."

Since Mom was about five feet nothing and ninety-five pounds she was very difficult to fit. It was almost a chore to go shopping for clothes with her. But what are good friends for? The task usually fell to Minnie. So periodically, when I was not available, Mom would contact Minnie or set it up the weekend before and off she would go on the subway again looking her usual snappy self, meet up with her friend and *schlepp* around from shop to shop of course stopping for a nice lunch. Seems like I'm doing the same things now.

Of course there were times that I was the designated partner. Somehow we made it fun especially when it came time for lunch and who should pay the bill. We took turns.

These friends, The Ladies, were a constant in Mom's life and in each other's. One husband would be in the hospital and somehow, miraculosly they would appear. When dad suffered a stroke Minnie was there the next day, arm around Mom.

We had a surprise seventy-fifth birthday party for Mom at my house and somehow everyone got here, by rides, buses, somehow.

Most of these women were my "Aunts" and therefore surrogate parents. Each one's passing were severe blows to my life and usually the only times I would see Mom cry.

The value of good friends can never be taken for granted. They remain in my memory bank forever.

JOSEPH WORZEL

Daddy

My Father emigrated to this country from Austria at age seven speaking only guttural Yiddish. He became deaf from two mastoids at age five. He was enrolled in the Lexington School for the Deaf and fortunately for him and the school, he was an excellent athlete excelling in track, basketball and baseball.

There seems to be several unifying bonds among the Deaf—as I said before, sports and card playing rank high on the list.

What mystery is it that without one of our major senses, deaf people excel in sports? Obviously there is much truth to the idea that when we lose one sense, the others are so keenly developed. My father could actually *hear* the lightning, sense a dog's barking, and *feel* music.

My Dad excelled in sports, provided for his family, and had an unbelievable lust for life. He also had an eye for beautiful women as was evidenced by his marrying my Mother.

Maybe I had a more of a special bond with my father than most young ladies. There's always the traditional father-daughter connection, but since my dad worked for a newspaper at night, he would be home during the day. Many Fridays we would take off to the three o'clock Ladies' Day games (in the days of daytime baseball.)

Opening baseball day in April was never missed and no excuse needed to skip school. The same would hold for the circus. Working for a newspaper had its advantages, one being free tickets to various events, (such as an occasional basketball game.) Sundays, when the annual Dodger-Giant rivalry was played out at the Polo Grounds, I would go with Daddy and take Mom's special lunch. There were always sandwiches, cookies and STUFF. I believe Mom used to go with Dad before I came along but fell asleep during a famous no-hitter, so I inevitably took her place. I also participated in the betting that went on with all his cronies. Once Dad caught three baseballs—in one game—barehanded, of course.

Besides Mom's STUFF no expense was spared for the EXTRAS: peanuts, hot dogs, ice cream, all the usual goodies. Dad believed a child should have everything she wanted at such events, otherwise why go?

I grew to love track and we would go to the annual Randall's Island track meets and see some of the track and field greats. I still have their autographs-athletes long gone like Greg Rice and Leslie McMitchell.

I remember visiting the '39 World's Fair with my folks and meeting the actress Helen Menken, who had deaf relatives. My parents were proud that someone famous was involved with the deaf.

He knew that Beethoven became deaf and gave me a recording of the fifth symphony. Dad said he could *feel* the *dot dot dot-dash* signifying V for Victory. He also was proud of the acheivments of Thomas Edison who had a hearing loss.

Dad showed me the importance of being well read and always made sure I had books, even comic books to read. Whenever I would be home from school with a cold or other malady he would bring me a Hardy Boy or Nancy Drew mystery and a box of Pine Brothers cough drops. It was a ritual. He would often help me with my homework. He taught me to subtract in a manner that to this day I do faster than anyone.

When I spent some time in Europe or in summer camp I would have a steady stream of wonderful letters that even now friends remember. When I returned home after a long trip, he had made a poster, THE PRODIGAL DAUGHTER HAS RETURNED.

Perhaps all this reading and writing had something to do with working in the newspaper business. Perhaps it has to do with being deaf and communication being so important. At any rate, reading has continued to be of importance to my family, and due to the closeness of my sons to their grandparents, so has writing.

My dad was intelligent, sharp, and funny—the joking kind of funny. Practical jokes were routine around our house. My father, the MASTER MAGICIAN with the disappearing coin trick that only fathers, grandfathers and old uncles seem to know. Pulling of the neck by the monster behind the door was another good one where he would stick his head in the room and make it seem as if someone else was pulling him by the neck.

Dad was 17 when he wrote this at the Lexington School for the Deaf. It's the best way to explain his background.

The Autobiography of Joe Worzel

I, a boy of Austrian-Jewish parentage, was born in Austria, a country in Europe, in the year 1898. There I dwelt in a wooden cottage with my parents and grandparents.

At the age of four, I was sent to school to be educated in the Austrian and Jewish languages. For nearly a year I studied very hard and learned how to speak these languages. Sometimes I was absent because of my desire to help my uncle who worked in a leather factory.

When the teacher received no report of my absence, he went to my house and spoke to my grandfather asking him why Yussel, a Jewish name for Joe, did not attend school the day before. Upon hearing this, my grandfather was very angry at me because I did not have his permission to help my uncle so he punished me very severely. (At that time, my parents were in America while I was left alone to live with my grandparents.)

At the age of five, I began to stop going to school on account of deafness and I lost my memory of speaking the Austrian and Jewish languages. Afterwards, I recovered my memory and was able to speak the common Jewish language.

I lived with my grandparents for two years. One day in our town, hundreds of buildings were consumed by fire and in the meantime, the people brought their bed blankets to the graveyard, as they believed that they would be saved from burning to death. My cousin and I did not go where the people went but walked several miles to another village where some of my relatives lived. We spent the night there.

On the next day, we returned to our town, finding many houses were completely destroyed and our house was one of them. After finding my grandparents in the graveyard, we all went to another cottage to live. It was very bad luck for my grandfather, for he had lost all his dairy products, hens and chickens, in the fire.

After that, I began to think of my parents who were residing in America, and wishing I was there, I asked my grandmother to write to my father and ask permission for me to come over there. At last after waiting for several months, I got my father's consent.

One morning, in the summer of 1905, my grandparents and I started off for America. We rode in a carriage from my house to the station, which was a few miles away. A few of my relatives and friends were waiting for us to bid us good-bye. We took a train for a town in Germany where my uncle was waiting for us. We had been on the train for two days, but at last we arrived in the town, We went to stay with my uncle for a few days. Then he escorted us to the station to take a train for a city somewhere in Germany, the name I have forgotten.

After our arrival in that city, we spent two days there. Before starting for America, we were vaccinated. It took us about two weeks to reach Brooklyn where my parents lived. It was a lonely trip as I could see nothing but water.

Upon arriving at Ellis Island, I found my father and mother there to take us home. I did not recognize them, for they had changed very much in appearance and neither did I recognize my sister when we arrived home.

At that time I had to put on American clothes. It was very strange to have them for the clothes here were very different from those of Austria.

Through all the summer I went to a doctor to see if he could make me hear, but he could not so he told my father that it was better to send his son to the 67th Street School for the Deaf. So this is how I came to be here. My father had the choice of sending me here or to Fanwood but he took the doctor's advice and sent me to this school. I am very glad that he did.

At that time I could speak only Yiddish but soon I became very much interested in the English language and it took me only a year to learn the alphabet. I like to study the language so I can talk to the other boys. It is a great delight to be here and go to the other towns to play ball. I like to ride on the cars and look out of the windows to see what are in the towns or talk with our boys. It is true that we never talk about the game on the day when we are in the train. After our victory or defeat, we then talk it all over.

Feb. 16, 1917

Joe Worzel
Would Have Played In The NBA

One night in 1957 in a Manhattan gym, the youth fourteen to sixteen year old basketball team of the Hebrew Association of the Deaf (HAD) had a game against the HAD old timers. No one remembers who won the game (the much experienced Old Timers did) or even the score. But fans attending the game would remember one thing - that Joe Worzel, attired in street clothes and dress shoes, entered the game with just a few seconds remaining and let go a set shot from midcourt. The ball went swish for a perfect basket!

The long range attempt itself was no big deal. What was the big deal was that Joe was 59 years old and had not played a game in years but was able to make the shot. How good was Joe as a basketball player when he was much younger?

Well, Joe was good enough to have played professional basketball, playing against some of the nation's most storied barnstorming teams of the twenties, playing for his Silent Separates team against the Original Celtics, the Rens and the Visitations among other long-forgotten teams.

And the late Art Kruger, the nation's most eminent sports writer for the deaf, chose Joe as the sixth greatest deaf player on his list of fifteen greatest deaf cagers of the half century (1900-1950), which was published in the January 1951 edition of the Silent Worker.

Art wrote "his remarkable accuracy in locating the basket made him a dangerous man and his speed in dribbling was a revelation." He had to be great in dribbling and shooting for he only weighed 115 lbs and could easily be shoved away by much-burlier opponents. Another asset that Joe had was his exemplary court sense - always making the right pass at the right moment for an opportune layup.

How good was he in AAAD ball? Unfortunately by the time AAAD came into existence (in 1945), Joe was too old to play competitive ball. That he was born too soon is a crying shame because the majority of deaf basketball fans have been denied a chance to see, and to marvel at, him in action. He would have run rings over everyones' fingers on the court.

Joe, born in Austria in 1898, became deaf at the age of seven after a bout of double mastoids. Emigrating to the States at the age of nine speaking only Yiddish. He enrolled at the Lexington School for the Deaf and it was there when he made a name for himself, not just in basketball, but also in baseball and in track and field.

After graduating from Lexington and before embarking on a long career as a printer for the New York Post he worked at his alma mater as a supervisor and then taught linotyping at the New York School for the Deaf. It was at the Post that he continued his association with basketball, getting free passes to pro games. He always stayed in touch with many of his old opponents, including Nat Holman and Joe Lapchick, these luminaries of old pro basketball days.

He has been inducted into two hall of fames - the AAAD (American Association Athletic of Deaf) and NCJD (National Congress of Jewish Deaf)

Daughter Lila Worzel Miller has inherited her father's athletic genes as she was inducted into the Brooklyn College athletic hall of fame. She attended the original NCJD hall of fame dinner at Philadelphia in 1984 to accept the honor on behalf of her deceased father. It was a tremendous thrill for her, but naturally she wished her father was alive to accept the honor in person.

Lila, who is not deaf, was quite an accomplished basketball player in her own right. Never mind the inherited genes, she has credited her father for making the person that she is. At present she is working on a book, a biography of her father, and is looking for a publisher. "I still take some shots at the basketball nowadays," she says. Don't ask her what her age is!

"Where have you gone Joe Dimaggio…
A nation lifts its lonely eyes to you-Boo-hoo-hoo-

Paul Simon

Renaissance Man

Most people think of my dad in relation to basketball. But to me it was baseball. My shared experiences with his cronies and participation in scoring and betting on the outcome of the games was special.

Dad was a sentimental softie. He couldn't hear, but the tears would stream down his face standing for the Star Spangled Banner at a ballgame. Whenever a dog or horse would die in a movie, oh boy! Guess I know whom I take after. Just seeing an old hero like Joe DiMaggio on TV would bring tears to my eyes and this year at his passing, it signified the end of an era.

I remember when I was about eight years old we received word that my Dad's mother, my grandmother, had passed away. Dad went into the living room, sat on the couch and quietly cried. I went to him sat on his lap and hugged him, simply a reflex action, I imagine. My aunt walked through the room and smiled, I don't know why, and Mom waved to Dad and said, "You should have gone last week." Since then I have never said to anyone, "You should have" about anything. I also never had much use for a man incapable of crying and respect a man who can.

Some years ago I was driving to work from the Bronx to Manhattan on the Major Deegan Highway. I pulled off the ramp and waited at the light. I looked to my right and there was Jackie Robinson in his white Caddy smiling at me and waving and flashing that beautiful grin. I was as excited as a teen-ager. Years later when I read Roger Kahn's "The Boys of Summer" I cried through the entire Jackie Robinson chapter. I guess I inherited my father's emotional side.

My Dad was A MAN FOR ALL SEASONS, a renaissance man. As I reflect on my life, I realize how remarkable he was. Bright, well read, a

wonderful athlete, a gambler at heart (I'm told his Father was a professional gambler), he loved card playing and the racetrack. My Mom and
Dad would trek to Yonkers raceway by bus about twice a week (he had
press passes from the New York Post) and invariably our conversation
when they got home went something like this:

"How'd you do?"

"Even!" (making the sign for 'even' much like the 'safe' sign in baseball.)

"Won $10."

"Broke!" (meaning lost, and making the sign, with the hand clipping
the neck.)

Now how did we survive the Depression? I'm told there was one, but
I certainly didn't know it. Dad had a job at The Home News, later
incorporated with the New York Post where he remained for over
thirty years. However, he started out as a substitute, waiting for a
'Permanent' job. In the meantime, he coached basketball at the New
York School for the Deaf (Fanwood) in White Plains. He would chal-
lenge other fellows for foul shots and One on One pickup games, and
played cards at the club (for money). I don't remember going hungry,
or wanting for anything.

Weekends in the summertime were a ritual. The Hebrew Association
for the Deaf had a bungalow in Far Rockaway called Camp Clark. Every
Saturday morning we were up bright and early. We rode the trolley over
the bridge to Washington Heights, walked (almost ran) in single file, Dad,
myself and Mom, all carrying clothes and lunch, up a steep hill to the
eighth Ave subway and downtown to catch the "8:53" at Pennsylvania
Station to Rockaway. Once there it was a communal dressing room, much

like the dressing rooms today at the beaches, then off to the beach for a day of fun.

Dad was a remarkable swimmer and loved diving into the waves. I developed a lifelong love of the beach and the ocean. Mom never learned to swim, but I remember her clutching my hands and the two of us jumping up and down over the waves. OH WHAT FUN WE HAD! She never let go and taught me respect for the ocean.

Did my father invent Root Beer Floats? I always thought so. We lived on the fourth floor of a walk-up apartment building. Even in the dead of winter, he would venture down in the evening and walk the five blocks to the grocery, buy a pint of ice cream and at home we would sit down, all three of us and make our Root Beer Floats, always with chocolate ice cream. Depression? Not for me.

I remember picnics with ball playing and food. We would gather with "The Crowd" deaf parents and a mixture of hearing and deaf children. We raced and played ball. The men usually organized a softball game, and I do remember my Father making a sensational catch in the outfield, Willie Mays style.

People used to say I looked just like my Mother, but reminded them of my Father in walk, running, and movement in general. Once while playing field hockey at Brooklyn College, one of his friends came over to me and signed, "Worzel's daughter?"

I was amazed and remember feeling rather proud, as Dad's friend had picked me out among all the girls. "How did you know?" I asked. "You look just like Joe."

We lived in the Bronx, but I went to Brooklyn College and was on the basketball team. We played all over the city, at New York University, Hunter College, City College, and of course at Brooklyn. Dad invariably showed up at the games. I would be playing and hello, he would appear, always signing, "GOOD PLAY." He got a kick that I was following in his footsteps, but always said, "Even better." I doubt it, but he would tell everyone about his daughter.

While I played in college, Dad taught me all the tricks of the trade. When you get pushed in a game, stumble, fall, anything to make sure you draw a foul. There was never a question about my making the foul shot. Another trick—when cornered, bounce the ball out of bounds off the opponent's foot. Your ball to inbound.

We practiced twice a week. My teammates and I would take the long train ride home from Brooklyn to the Bronx. It might be 8:30 or 9 at night. I would get off the train, walk up the long flight of steps and there he would be, Daddy, waiting to walk his baby home. He knew the approximate time I would arrive, never mind that it might be the dead of winter.

My husband and I accompanied Mom one weekend to Philadelphia for an award ceremony. Dad was being inducted into the National Deaf Hall of Fame (posthumously) for his achievements in sports (particularly basketball) both as player and Coach. (After his playing days, he became the Coach for the Hebrew Association of the Deaf team.)

The Master of Ceremonies spoke of Dad and his playing prowess. How Dad had once showed him how to "Sink" some baskets from mid-court. He said, "At that time, he was 65." Well, here I am, at that age, so I guess I had better move the basket closer (and maybe even lower).

Like father like daughter, I was inducted into the Brooklyn College Sports Hall of Fame for Basketball in 1981. Dad would have been so proud. I could see his chest swell with pride and with his fist, exclaim—"Yes! Yes! Yes!"

My husband and father got along fabulously. They would tease, joke and try to one-up on each other. My dad was an ardent Republican. (He liked to think of himself as a rich bon-vivant, the Jimmy Walker type.) My husband is a Democrat. He and dad once got into a heated debate over the coming election. It started in good fun, but got extremely frustrating for my Dad, who I might add, had a temper. Rather than continue and get angry, he simply took off his glasses and closed his eyes. After about 30 seconds, he opened his eyes slightly, and peeked out at my husband who had already removed his own glasses. It was quite a sight, and they both broke up with laughter.

When I graduated from College, I taught for one year, then travelled to Europe with a friend. I returned and lived at home. I did some substitute teaching enough to pay the rent and in between got an old car played golf and had a good time. The neighbors would question Dad, "What's with her?"

"She's fine, it's o.k."

That was my Father.

CHAPTER 4

Family and Friends

Influences

My folks influenced many people throughout their lives. Dad was able to secure positions into the printer's union for several young men, a much sought after privilege at that time. Newspapers wanted deaf men as the sound of the printing presses didn't bother them and they proved to be good workers.

My husband's niece Nancy, is a Speech Pathologist. Nancy was eight when she met my parents. They took a special liking to each other and by the time she was ten she knew she would pursue a career in Speech and Communicative Disorders.

Socializing with my folks gave her "a level of comfort with handicap people."

Her daughter Cally, is now at college in Ohio and studying Sociology and reading about different make-ups of family units.

So, we hopefully in our lifetime affect each other in some way.

George

I was calling for my new date at her home and rang the doorbell. The door was opened by my future father-in-law who smiled, said, "Hello" and with a flourish, graciously escorted me into the living room. I didn't know that he was deaf; I didn't know that the doorbell was connected to a light bulb that lit up when the bell was rung.

Lila came into the room, her father said goodbye, nice to meet you and left. Lila introduced me to her mother who responded with a sweet smile and a few words of greeting.

It was only later during the evening that I realized that these perfectly normal parents reacting to their daughter's new date were supposed to have a handicap!!!?

This was my first meeting with deaf people—and it impressed me a great deal. As my father–in–law said a few years later with a knowing grin, he certainly conned me at our first meeting; it was an awakening.

Lila's mother Miriam was a lady. She was always concerned for other people and was involved in her various group activities. Her daughter, of course, was the apple of her eye, and I, by proxy, became her favorite also.

I remember the first time I had dinner at her home. Miriam went all out to make sure I would enjoy the meal. Sweet potatoes, vegetables, pot roast cooked, 'just so.' "Did I enjoy the pot roast?" she asked. Courteously, I replied that I did—and so, for the next thirty five years, whenever Miriam served me a meal—you guessed it-it was pot roast.

Lila has written about her father's and my political (friendly) differences and discussions. They were fun and stimulating. But I remember other wonderful moments. When our first son, Howard was born he so proudly pushed the baby carriage waving everyone away. This was HIS grandson and you had better not interfere. When Lila went back to teaching and we both had to leave early in the morning, Joe was the first to arrive to baby-sit and always in plenty of time. Miriam came along later. This would be his playtime alone and later the same with Andy. He fed Howard, dressed him and loved every minute of his "job." He also was the first to realize Howard was a 'lefty' and got a kick out of it, thinking along the lines of the southpaw greats of baseball.

One memory that stands out is the time I was driving Miriam and Joe to our summer bungalow. Joe had just had carotid artery surgery and was coming up to recuperate. Determined to follow his doctor's advice to exercise, he had me stop the car at a rest stop so that he could walk around and around the car for a few minutes. Of course I had been given those orders by Lila before I started out. It was a funny sight to behold, the two of us in the car and Joe walking round and round.

When Howard was born I hurried to my in-laws to tell them the good news. It was about ten p.m. and before they had a TTY. They weren't home and the reason would become a long standing joke. Where were they? At the Trotters at Yonkers Raceway, of course. Soon I saw their shadows emerge from the darkness. Joe spotted me and started to run to me and I to him. I signed from the distance—it's a boy! He turned to Miriam and gave the sign for hooray and a boy. They hugged each other, then me and we all danced around with glee at my first child and their first grandchild.

Whenever we would go for a drive there was no arguing about who would pay the toll. Joe always had the exact change out and never you mind.

They were good people-my in-laws-my friends.

Nancy

I am a doctor of speech and language disorders. The fact that I am a doctor is not that surprising as I am bright and neurotically focused. However, the fact that I knew that I would be concentrating in the field of communicative disorders since the age of ten is surprising. I have often asked myself how I knew my ultimate goal from such a young age, and find myself returning to the first time I met my aunt's parents.

I remember meeting them when we watched my aunt and uncle get married on television. Being eight years old, I was fascinated by my aunt and uncle who were about to become stars on the television program "Bride and Groom." But I found myself distracted from the television cameras to be drawn to stare at my new aunt's parents. They were talking but only partially with their mouths. Their hands were flying and the sounds were different. I noticed too that my new aunt changed voice quality to match the tone of her parents' when she spoke and signed to them. I was also intrigued by my aunt's father's easy smile. He seemed approachable and despite the fact that I was warned not to stare, when I did, he smiled. He understood my sense of fascination and instead of being embarrassed by my curiosity he was open about it,

In fact, he quickly reached into his pocket and gave me a card with the manual alphabet. I memorized the card, which I have saved, along with others that he gave me, and gave them to my friends and eventually to my daughters. The next time I met my aunt's parents I shyly spelled out words. They encouraged me and did not make me feel uncomfortable. I proceeded to teach my friends and we had a new secret language for school. I remember one day when I was proud of my accomplishments. I was signing with my uncle during synagogue and I overheard someone say, "How sad, she is deaf." I was so proud of myself.

Whenever the family got together, I spoke with my aunt's parents. When I was in high school I did some volunteer work at the Lexington School for the Deaf once a week. I was comfortable with the students as a result of my interaction with my Aunt's parents. While I did not go on to study Deaf Education, as Queens College did not have a major in that area, I did go on to study in the field of communicative disorders, first becoming a speech therapist and then going on for my doctorate. Currently, I work with the autistic population, my most challenging cases being those children with severe auditory processing difficulties, teaching them not only to talk but to listen—something my aunt's parents could do despite their lack of hearing.

Ida and Bertye

Mom had two sisters, my Aunt Ida and Aunt Bertye, both hearing. They saw to it that I was exposed to every possible cultural experience. Ida took me to my first opera. It was at Lewisohn stadium, a memory of the past located at the site of City College. I remember hearing La Boheme and my aunt getting a big kick listening to me afterwards humming the music to Carmen, not Boheme (the Toreador song probably being one of the first classical tunes a child learns.) It was the start of many events at Lewisohn Stadium and my generation will never forget the memorable Minnie Guggenheimer and her rousing speeches.

We saw major performers for less than a dollar performed at this huge amphitheater.

My Aunt Ida took me to my first concert and my Aunt Bertye to my first Broadway play. Bertye and I would thereafter regularly attend many Broadway plays year after year.

Since the theater contained much of what would now be called R-rated I was exposed at an early age to a level of sophisticated comedy.

Bertye at some time in my early childhood lived with Mom and Dad. I suspect it was mutual, Bertye contributing financially and Mom having the benefit of her sister around and eventually my getting use of a phone, since Bertye was single and could hear.

Bertye got married when I was in my teens and moved to California. I remember Mom crying. But it was tears for happiness, I'm sure.

Unfortunately, it didn't work out and Bertye moved back to New York and got her own apartment nearby. She was certainly an extension of our family. The sisters had a brother, my Uncle Abe, who lived in New Jersey, and it was mainly due to Bertye that the closeness of the family was maintained. Bertye would call and make arrangements for all of us to go visit. Abe had a chicken farm and it was there that I learned how to candle eggs. Abe offered Mom a hearing aid time after time, but whenever she tried one on it only made her nervous, so she managed without one.

They also had another brother, Izzy who died when I was very young.

Ida and Bertye took me on my first roller coaster ride, THE CYCLONE, in Coney Island. I was about eight, turned green and threw up when I got off. Mom always remembered that. She was smart and waited down below.

Bertye would sometimes take me along on her dates. She always told me to make sure I called her Aunt, lest anyone think she was my mother.

As long as I can remember my Aunt Ida was married to my Uncle Nicholas. Theirs is a love story I will address in my next book. They had a house upstate from us and we went there many weekends. When I had my own family we all got to enjoy apple picking and learned something about farming.

Ida eventually moved to Florida and kept up a correspondence with Mom that forever intrigued me since they couldn't communicate by phone. They wrote periodically and always signed their letters with a loving Sis Ida or Sis Miriam.

Ida was my **Aunt** Ida until I was way past fifty. Then I began to call her just Ida in person and in letters. It seemed a natural progression and it was fine with her. At that point she still had my sons call her aunt.

It was my Aunt Ida who was constantly reminding me of the proprieties in life, like writing thank you notes, which I am always reminding my sons to do.

It is through my parents of course, but my aunts as well, who played a major role in teaching me a sense of responsibility and the importance of family.

Jerry

Jerry was my mother's first cousin, their mothers having been sisters. He was considerably younger than mom and older than I.

He filled in, between my aunts, in transporting me to all venues of culture and sports.

He played tennis, skated, but his first love was theater and so it became ingrained in me, and remains to this day. After World War II and a little short of money, he would go to the second act of every Broadway show managing to find an empty seat (a trick I manage to do in movie theaters for a second movie much to the chagrin of my children who are expecting to bail me out of jail any day.)

He was in the army during World War II and I clearly remember his last home meal at our house. My mom cried and he said, "Don't worry, I won't get killed."

My friend and I were twelve and walked him to the subway to say goodbye. I received wonderful V-Mail letters from him that brought me closer to the realities of the War.

Fortunately he came home in one piece, decided to try his luck in Japan having had enough of Europe, worked for the government, married Nachino, a Japanese woman he met, and raised Kathy, their daughter, the same Kathy who is now an integral part of this story. So, it may not take a village to raise a child, but family around for support certainly is a lucky thing to have.

The Crowd

Much of my parents' social life revolved around the H.A.D. (Hebrew Association of the Deaf.) The men had their weekly card games, the women their monthly sisterhood. There were social functions such as dinner-dances and New Years' Eve. parties and in general, good times. The ladies annual Mother-Daughter luncheons were a particular treat. Mom and I, for many years, won the "Most-who-look-alike contest."

My parents main comraderie and friendships, however, came from THE CROWD in particular. These were five couples that were friends for as long as I can remember. Many of them went back as far as public school (1918-1923). They did everything and went everywhere together. They took turns for the Saturday evening get-togethers and once or twice a year, The Crowd went up to Harry and Flo's country house where they lived most of the time. Somehow or other I seemed to be the only youngster included and boy, do I remember the good times. I remember everyone going home with a box of delicious cookies and jars of pickled herring and lox. I remember summers and winters, ice-skating, sleigh-riding, swimming and boating. This was Harry and Flo's way of taking their turn at hosting.

These friends were together through thick and thin, good and bad times. Truthfully, they were mostly good. When my Dad was in the hospital, it was these friends that came each day and sat with Mom to give her comfort.

In fact one of the couples is buried next to mom and dad so they can play cards forever.

On occasion, Miriam and Joe would go up to the country alone, without the other couples to visit with Harry and Flo. I would go along,

being too young to stay home alone. This made for a special relationship with their children, Sandy and Mary Ann and me. We would play
and tease each other, and carry on like devils. I think we generally took
advantage of the fact that our folks were deaf and we tried to "get away
with murder" as my mother used to say.

I remember my Mother saying, "We are going up to the country. Be
nice and play with Mary Ann and Sandy. We are guests. Behave!"

"Phooey! They're younger than I am," I would reply.

Flo would tell Mary Ann to be nice and play with me. "Company is
coming. Be good!"

"Phooey! I want to play with my own friends!"

Somehow, however, in spite of all these objections, we managed to
survive the weekends and even have a good time.

My folks enjoyed many things but card playing was number one, be
it with friends, our family and or our kids when they were older.

Horseracing, particularly the Trotters was number two on the list of
pleasures.

Once, at Yonkers Raceway, a favorite of theirs, someone tapped my
Dad on the back. He turned around and, GOODNESS! It was ED SUL-
LIVAN, then quite prominent on TV (besides having a column in the
newspaper every day).

"Do you remember me?" Ed Sullivan asked my father.

Of course he did. Way back in their younger days, they had played
basketball against each other along with Nat Holman, Joe Lapchick and
other notables. I don't know if my folks won or lost that night, but who
cared? Dad had plenty of stories to tell that week. Some of the crowd
enjoyed the horse racing, all loved cards, some basketball but mostly
they loved each other. This unique generation has passed on but the values they gave me are forever.

Uncle Joe

I recently attended a family function on my father's side. I spoke to my cousin Harold, now seventy-five years old. He told me many stories about "Uncle Joe" that I had never heard.

"He used to take me to the "Club" every weekend and I'd watch him play cards. Sometimes he'd give me a quarter (a good deal of money in those days) and I'd get ice cream or some other goody. Other times, he'd take me to watch him play basketball, or to baseball games. He was a terrific athlete."

"Why did he do this?" my husband and I asked?

"I was his sister's son. He was very good to me."

Our eyes started to fill up. Nevertheless, he continued. "When he started to date Miriam, he would take me along on weekends. We would even go to the movies. He always had pad and pencil ready. He never considered himself handicapped. In a restaurant he would be able to order. He was very good to me," he repeated.

"I never knew anything was wrong with him. He was just my Uncle Joe," said my cousin Harold.

This conversation prompted me to call Harold's older sister in California, who I knew took care of me when I was born.

"I have plenty of stories," Alice said. "Remember, I was the first child. Uncle Joe taught me the manual alphabet when I was three. He told me, "If you forget the signs for the words, you'll always remember the alphabet."

Of all the cousins, Alice was and still is the most proficient at sign.

It was nice to find out about this history between my cousins and my folks.

CHAPTER 5

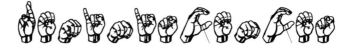

Reminiscences

Nice Things

One thing about Mom was her penchant for "Nice Things." She was quite the lady when it came to propriety and "Fancy Stuff."

Everyone would always comment on how proper and perfect Miriam looked and how her apartment was to a T and everything in place.

At times I would ask if it was possible that I was adopted as I was so different. (We'd both crack up at that, after winning the Mother-daughter look-alike contest at the H.A.D. luncheon every year.) It's not that I was careless or sloppy, but definitely not a neatnik.

The everyday plain napkins weren't good enough for Mom. She liked her Vanity Fair special napkins. And no plain milk in her coffee, mind you. It was always "Half and Half." And while in a restaurant, when we'd have ice-cream with whipped cream for dessert and coffee, she would carefully spoon the cream into her coffee a little at a time, and look up and beam, "French Coffee."

Mom love elegant restaurants and definitely enjoyed a cocktail. She would want to know the latest 'in' drink. First it was a Brandy Alexander, then an Amaretto Sour. She would take a sip, smack her lips and give a thumbs up smile.

I recently had an Amaretto Sour and had fond feelings of nostalgia.

Mom would never interfere with our family regarding my child-rearing and personal business. But, on occasion, when she came to our house for a few days, invariably the words would come out, "If you don't mind my saying so, the curtains need cleaning." Or, "The boys shouldn't leave the table until we're all done," and so on.

You can bet that when she came up I had Vanity Fair napkins and "Half and Half".

Whenever we would need something for Grandma, we could always count on Crabtree and Evelyn soaps. She loved the smell and texture of fancy soaps. Me, I'm allergic!

As I said, I was never truly aware of a depression. When Mom made her spaghetti croquettes (to this day, I've never known anyone that has heard of that) it never occurred to me that it was a leftover dish. And didn't everyone cover their schoolbooks with cut up paper bags? Once in a while, Mom and I used oilcloth to cover the books. It wasn't until much later that I discovered the special covers with the name of your school imprinted on the cover. FANCY!!

Later on, when I was teaching in the Bronx, every now and then, I would spend the evening with Mom and sleep over. Just the two of us. I would get there after three p.m. Milk and cookies were waiting and always, a dish of "Andes" candies. Then came a nap, and after, we would have a nice quiet dinner together or go out to a nearby diner or for Chinese food. We'd watch TV until late, sleep, and the next morning my breakfast would be ready and certainly a nice lunch packed. Even if I knew I was going out for lunch, I wouldn't deprive Mom of her fussing over me.

My husband and I used to have a concert subscription in New York. On those nights, we would both have dinner with Mom and sleep over to save us the trip home, but more to visit. Those were good times. Going to the concerts now just isn't the same.

Sex

Sex talks between mothers and daughters, or fathers and sons back then (in the olden days) were slightly different than today. Our children would find it all very funny.

I remember I was eleven or twelve (which in itself is funny as kids today learn about sex at four or five) when one day Mom said to me, "Do you know about it?" I smiled and said, "Yes." End of discussion.

I actually learned the facts of life sitting on the stoop of my apartment house from two older boys (maybe fourteen). That actual *word* was what you did to get a baby. OUR PARENTS? Impossible!

Truthfully, to give Mom her due, she gave me this bit of advice. "Remember, it's always the girls' fault. Be careful. No leading a boy on. Of course, if anything should happen to you, *remember*, you come right home! We'll take care of you."

Quite the modern woman, don't you think?

On the other hand, my kids could always talk to Grandma about sex. Once Howard asked Grandma if she thought so and so (a couple past 75) still did IT? "Why not?" she answered.

My younger son, Andy once asked her if he wasn't right in seeing many different young ladies rather than going steady with just one? Sure mom agreed and proceeded to give him advice.

When I was grown up and married however, Mom did say to me, "Dirty jokes! That's all deaf people talk about. Do hearing people do the same thing?"

"Oh yes, Mom."

There is a certain indefinable quality of bonding between grandparents and grandchildren that is something special.

Romance

There's sex and there's romance. I don't know if I was born an incurable romantic, but I think those of us who spent hours watching the movies of the forties and fifties had to have been seduced by them. How could you not with movies like "THREE COINS in the FOUNTAIN," "The GHOST and MRS. MUIR," " LOVE is a MANY SPLENDORED THING," and everyone's favorite, "CASABLANCA." And how about Paul Henreid lighting two cigarettes with one match in "NOW VOYAGER?"

Yesterdays are so important. Mom and I would go to the movies together and I would get a kick out of her smiles at the current heroes. She would nudge me and say, "He's good looking." Usually I agreed. Mom used to tell me about all the old movie stars and give me that wicked grin. Once she took me to see an old John Barrymore film. I grinned along with her.

For her it was Barrymore and Valentino, but of course we both had Cary Grant for whom there may never be a replacement.

When I was very young Mom took me to see Pride And Prejudice with (Gasp) Laurence Olivier. I walked out of the theater in such a trance that Mom had to hold on to me as a trolley car was coming. (Yes that long ago.)

Yet there were times when we were at the movies and I'd laugh at a joke and mom would say, "What?" I'd wave, "Later" selfishly wanting to hear the whole line first. I do regret that I wasn't more proficient at simultaneously listening and signing.

Happily, Mom never lost her sense of romance. Late in life when she was alone, she started to read the latest love novels. I do believe this kept her going. Vivé la Romance!

Courage

Mom broke her hip just before her 83rd birthday. A stay in the hospital is traumatic enough for anyone, but for a person with a handicap, oh boy! One would think in this day and age, hospital personnel would understand the needs of older persons. But they would take Mom's glasses off at night and between not being able to see nor hearing it got quite rough. But Mom got through it.

It took a month, then another in a rehab facility. When Mom came home, she had a lovely young lady, Sherrill living in to assist. They got along well. Mom did her best with a visiting therapist, but was really fearful of walking. She did try and try, up and down the hallway and around and around the apartment.

My husband and I would stay over on weekends to give her young lady time off and try to make it more pleasant for both Mom and us.

One special time when I was relieving Sherrill on Mother's Day, Mom and I went out for breakfast to the nearby McDonald's. She thought it was so nice that they gave flowers to all the Moms. It was a real Mother-daughter outing. For all we knew, it could have been Tavern on the Green. Funny, but that's the Mother's Day I remember most. I got to be a daughter again.

Need

After Mom became ill, first breaking her hip, then suffering a stroke, I of course became the caregiver. But now and then I would need to become a child again and my Mother's daughter. Occasionally I would try devious methods to gain attention and sympathy. Once I really had hurt my foot, a stress fracture. Well, did I milk that! I would limp in, my foot in a bandage with one of those soft orthopedic shoes. I desperately needed to have my Mother be concerned for me. I didn't think I was being selfish. I wanted to divert her attention away from her own problems. It did work. For several weeks after, she would always ask, "How's your foot?" Then she would laugh. I think she knew what I wanted.

Mom had a wonderful acceptance of life. She always said to me, "Don't worry, one day I'll go to sleep and that will be that."

The phone call came at two a.m. I jumped up, my heart racing instantly, knowing what it had to be.

It was Audrey, Mom's evening caregiver. "I think she's gone. I called 911." "How did you know?" I asked. "I heard a gasp (I imagine Audrey had been through this before with other clients) and went to look at her. I don't think she's breathing."

Mom kept her promise. She died as sweetly, gently and uncomplaining as she lived. Our 62 years together were all too short.

Surprises

Mom was full of surprises, but at this advanced time of her life, dependent, and we feeling stressful most of the time, it was always a wonder to us how the littlest smile or remark from her would make our day.

One night she called after she had broken her hip.

"It's Sherrill's birthday and I would like to take her out for Chinese food. Do you think it's okay to ask Sadie (her neighbor next door) to lend me $20?"

"Yes," I answered quickly. I was actually thrilled that Mom took this initiative. Later she related to me, in detail, as she always did what they ate and all the intricacies of getting there and back.

"We had fun!" Mom said. Mom usually had fun.

Once she won $3 at her club in a drawing. That was on a Wednesday, the usual club day when I would take her over to see some other people. When we came home I showed her the money and put it in her drawer for anything special that might come arise.

A week later my son Andy visited Grandma. He asked Grandma to massage his feet, a ritual between them. She noticed that he wasn't wearing any socks.

"No socks!" she exclaimed, her hands spread apart, as if to say, "Why?"

"I'm poor," he signed, making the sign for poor, taking one hand and pulling at the elbow of the other to show the need for patches.

"Where's the $3 I won?" Mom asked me.

I almost fainted. All three of us, my husband, Mom's home attendant and I were speechless.

I jumped up, got the money and gave it to her.

"Here," she said, "Go buy yourself some socks." Mom was beaming. She knew she just blew us away.

We decided to surprise Mom once and brought Cricket to visit. Mom was laughing and calling, "Cricket, don't you want to see Grandma?" Cricket not being used to the city was pacing up and down anxious to get out of there. We took her to the lobby and the neighbors kept calling to her. Mom explained that of course Cricket was deaf also. Everyone got a laugh out of that, so indeed, Cricket's visit was a success.

I always knew Mom was proud of me. She would correct me from time to time while I was growing up, and even as an adult. When we would go to her mother-daughter luncheons, she would warn me in advance, "If you please, wear a skirt."

Mom knew I usually wore slacks. She was however, always ready with a compliment. Praise is certainly important to a child growing up, but maybe it's something special when the child is an adult, and even more so when your parent is aging and the occasional spark comes to life.

One Saturday my husband and I visited Mom. I had asked her home attendant to take Mom to the Sabbath services that morning, as a diversion for her and to see other people. I was somewhat obsessed with other people seeing Mom and their knowing she was still okay. I don't believe Mom cared one way or the other.

Mom and I said hello in the midst of the service. Mom signed, "It's long."

I signed, "Almost finished."

Then the young Rabbi called on me to hold up the Torah while he removed the cover, an honor. I went up, held it and took a peek at Mom. WELL! You would think I had taken my first step. The smile on her face told me everything. I was still the daughter, she the Mom and she was PROUD! The word in Yiddish is KVELL—and boy did she. Now who got the most out of that visit, I ask you?

Mom's Diaries

Once for her birthday, my son Howard gave his Grandma a five year diary.

"What shall I put in it? What shall I write about?" Grandma asked. Howard said, "Anything you want. Good things, bad things, your thoughts, anything." Later after he left, Mom repeated," What shall I put in it? What shall I write about?"

"Anything you want. Put down your thoughts," I said.

I discovered Mom did just that. And she wrote just as she spoke, in detail. Mom would never only say, "I went to the movies." Rather it would be, "I took the bus, which came late. I had to wait and wait, in the cold, and I almost missed the beginning, etc, etc."

She wrote only good things, usually on her birthday, when we would do something special, and on days when something unusual happened. I get a kick out of reading them now and share some of that with you. I have selected some entries at random.

"This diary given to me from my grandson, Howard Scott Miller, January, 1985."

"January 11, 1985."

Spent a lovely weekend with my daughter Lila and son-in-law George in New City, 11th Friday till Sunday 13th. Saturday, the day was sunny and cold. We didn't feel like going out. Took a nap late afternoon and around 5:30 p.m., Cricket barked and barked, hence George went to the front door and took a bundle from a delivery boy. Said that it was for me. A surprise when I saw a bouquet of beautiful flowers from Howard and Andy. Aren't my grandsons lovable and thoughtful! They presented me with a brand new television with remote control for my birthday. Surely enjoy watching TV every night. Saturday evening, Lila and George took me out to dinner in Nyack. Sunday, 13th, brunch at 1pm in Westchester. Fancy restaurant and it was very crowded. My neighbors, Sadie and Manny joined us. Buffet table from shrimps, salad, eggs, meat, coffee, cake and ice cream. After three hours, time to go home. Went home with Sadie and Manny with the flowers which stayed alive about 3 weeks. Lila and George gave me a Teletype Minicom II for my birthday. It is a pleasure that I can make contact with friends through TTY back and forth.

"January 13th, 1986."

Howard and Andy sent me a beautiful bouquet of flowers on my birthday, and on 14th, Lila took me to a French restaurant on 50th St., then walked to 45th St. to see the show, "Song and Dance." We had a seat first row in orchestra. It was very good and dancing colorful and different. Everyone had to get out early. It was freezing, 15 degrees, waiting for a cab and finally took us straight home. We had coffee and cookies and watched television till 1:00 a.m. Poor Lila had to get up early to go to work. I'm sure that she'll be glad to retire this June.

"January 18th, 1986."

Took a cab to my cousin Kathy Friedman's office, West 34th St. and went up in elevator to 14th floor. The office is small and a little crowded but she said that in a few weeks she will move up to a larger one on 28th floor. She has six girls working with her. Then we took a cab to her apt. on 15th St., waiting for her husband, Alan. We walked to a restaurant nearby and had a good lunch. Again, took a cab to see the movie, "White Nights." Not bad!

We bought lottery tickets for 30 million dollars, though we were out. A lucky couple from Staten Island won. Back to the apt. and Kathy called up car service to take me home. She wouldn't let me pay and gave me money for the driver. Got home around 7:30p.m. What a day! Anyway, enjoyed it very much.

"April 4, 1985."

Lila, George and I flew to San Francisco to spend a week with Howard and Andy. Friday morning we drove to Berkeley to have lunch, then walked around the town. Time to go back to Howard's apt. to prepare dinner for the first seder. He invited two girls, one American, the other Japanese from where he works. Dinner was delicious, from soup to dessert.

The girls stayed till 1a.m. Saturday morn, we drove around and walked till 5p.m. Andy and I flew to Los Angeles, a one hour ride. Then to Andy's apt. with 2 boys and 3 bedrooms. Sunday, Andy and I drove to Venice Beach and had lunch there. Walked around till late afternoon then back home and rested for a while. In the evening, I took Andy out to dinner and after dinner, Andy drove me to my niece, Alice, in Hollywood-stayed with her 2½ days-Andy picked me up Wednesday eve., back to his apt. and stayed overnight. Up early Thursday morn to take flight back to San Francisco to meet Lila and George going home. Three ½ hours to Newark. Then a friend of theirs drove me home. A perfect week—not even one rainy day.

July, 1984:

Lila, George and I flew to San Francisco to visit Howard. His apartment very lovely with his friend with 2 bedrooms, 2 baths, small kitchen and a large living room. Andy joined us too. One day Andy and I took a ferry to Alcatraz and walked around the island. No prisoners there. A lady guide explained the story about the prisoners, how they were treated, cruel and mean. The prison was closed in 1963 but the tourists can visit there if they want.

Back to Howard's home and out to dinner.

July 18-Bus ride to Yosemite with Lila and George. Car ride around 2 hours.

July 19-Back to San Francisco

July 20-to Hawaii with Lila and George, Howard and Andy. First stop to Honolulu. Then to Oahu, Kawai, and Maui. Visited all the beaches and towns, very interesting. Grand time had by all of us. Lila and George and I came home second week in August.

My next trip-to where???

CHAPTER 6

Memories

My Grandparents

Howard Miller

My earliest recollection that I have that about my grandparents is that they sounded different than other adults. When I was about four years old my younger brother and I nicknamed our grandmother 'witch' and our grandfather 'monster' because that is what they sounded like to us. Grandma's voice was funny from being hard of hearing, so it seemed like a witch. Grandpa was stone deaf and couldn't talk and when he verbalized it sounded like a ghost or monster.

While we called them witch and monster, we weren't afraid of them. In fact, we looked forward to their visits, especially when they babysat for us! My brother and I thought we were cool kids because after they put us to bed we stayed up screaming and yelling. They couldn't hear us! When they would come into our rooms we pretended to be asleep. Looking back, it makes me laugh knowing we actually thought we were pulling something over on them!

Deaf my grandparents were, but dumb they certainly weren't. They both forged fruitful lives for themselves and their daughter despite their deafness.

I didn't know my grandfather that well. He spent more time with my younger brother when my mother went back to work and I went to school. I would see him when the family got together and he died before I had the chance to appreciate the bonus of having grandparents.

However, I certainly got to know my grandma since she lived a good twenty years after my grandpa passed away.

Grandma was always independent and very active. I don't think she took the risks or dares she might have wanted to take as she got older (dating again, doing volunteer work) but she kept very busy up until her accident five years before she died.

Grandma was a joy to be around. When we were in high school, at our rebellious stage I certainly had problems with my parents and my brother. I'm sure my brother had the same parent and sibling issues, and my parents had their family issues, as well.

However, one thing we all agreed on was our grandma. She didn't judge, and rarely complained. When grandma would come to visit for the weekend (which wasn't all the time since her social calendar quickly filled) we would all take time out from what we were doing to spend time with her.

Grandma was a card player and my brother and I would spend a good deal of time playing casino or crazy eights with her. It was fun to see my grandmother focus so intently and take the game so seriously.

Our family dog, Cricket, also loved her. You might say Cricket loved everyone, but she got especially excited when grandma would come to visit.

My father loved his mother in law. It was a common joke in our family that my father didn't call my grandmother by name. He certainly didn't call her mom, or Miriam, or Mrs. Worzel. He would refer to her as Lila's mom. But he always treated her as one of the family.

Many of my peers in high school complained about their grandparents, how they drove them crazy and they didn't want to be around them. I never understood this. It was the opposite for me. When Grandma was around, the pressure was off. My parents were more relaxed (for the most part) and everyone got along, no matter what the arguments were prior to her visit.

I don't know if my relationship with my grandmother was anything different then anyone else who had a great relationship with their grandparent. I didn't have this relationship because she was hard of hearing, I had it because of who she was.

I don't believe that my mother had as perfect relationship with her parents as her book states. Every child has issues with their parents. Either my mother has forgotten her issues, grew past them, or chose to ignore them. But I would think being a hearing child for deaf parents would have its burden on a child. Plus, I grew up knowing that while my grandfather let my mother do anything she wanted, my grandmother was quite strict with her. I wonder whether my mother would have an opinion on that.

The last few years of my grandmother's life wasn't typical of most of her years. A broken hip, a few mild strokes made her dependent on others for help, and sunk her spirit and will to live. But I would go visit her everytime I was in New York. We would play cards as we always did. A little slower pace, but she remembered the games.

This past summer, over five years since my grandmother passed away, I was in New York with a free afternoon to spare. I thought about what I wanted to do and I realized I wanted to take the train and visit my grandma. While I can't do that anymore, I am comforted that she will be alive inside me forever.

Andy on Grandma

My son, Andy delivered the eulogy at Mom's funeral.

Miriam Worzel was born Miriam Robin on January 13, 1905 the youngest in a family of two boys and three girls. Her Dad left her Mom when she was young, taking the two boys with him. "I can never call him my Father," Miriam used to say, "He's just the old man."

She attended the Lexington School for the Deaf in Manhattan, graduating with the class of '23. There she met Joseph Worzel and after they had been seeing each other for a while, Miriam turned to him one time and said, "Listen, I think it's time we get married." They did in 1928.

They had one child, Lila, who they raised during the Depression, a time we know was tough for all, but I can only imagine must have been extremely difficult for two "Deaf" parents.

But Lila never knew of their struggle. At least not when she was young. Miriam and Joe managed just fine, living, in fact, a very broad life. They travelled all over the world. They saw shows, movies, took trips to the country. They lived life and anyone who knew Miriam Worzel can testify to that.

Lila married George, Howard and I were born, and we lived only a few blocks away from my grandparents. During elementary school, we would eat lunch at their house and a real bond was formed.

I always thought all grandparents were deaf. It used to amaze me, and still does, when a friend of mine would be able to simply "talk" to his grandparent. One couldn't just "talk" to Miriam. It took some effort, which made it all that more special.

Joe Worzel died 25 years ago, and I remember my Grandmother holding me in her arms, telling me, "We must be brave."

Miriam was always brave. She spoke her mind, but always kept it open. She was as liberal as they get and I found I was always able to speak to her about anything—anything.

We talked of death once, several years ago, and I asked her if she feared dying. She thought for a moment, really thought, and then shook her head. I think my Grandmother was more concerned with living.

The last few years weren't kind to Miriam. She broke her hip, had a series of strokes and was ultimately confined to a wheelchair, unable to care for herself. Miriam would drift in and out of reality, but then I learned a little of her "fantasy world" and got to know her even better.

She rarely complained, and the thing I'll remember most is her smile. For if I had to describe Miriam Worzel, I would describe her smile. It was warm, sincere, full of love and joy…full of life. What made the last couple of years bearable has been this smile, which she always flashed to the end.

Miriam died at age 87 and leaves behind a sister, Ida, age 92, who is now living in Florida, temporarily displaced by Hurricane Andrew. Ida is an incredible woman and as the eldest sister, helped to raise Miriam. I can only imagine the bond these two shared, and my Aunt Ida, when I saw her a few weeks ago, told me to tell Miriam that she loved her very, very much. I told Miriam and each time I told her she smiled her smile.

Miriam also left behind her son-in-law, George. I never knew a guy who loved his Mother-in-law more. And she loved him.

There's Howard and myself and for both of us, the word "Grandma" only means good things.

And of course there's her daughter, Lila. Miriam and Lila took turns taking care of each other throughout their lives, argued and yelled, shopped and laughed. They were more than Mother and Daughter, they were friends.

Let's not feel sorry for my Grandmother, or for ourselves. Her struggle is over, and wherever she is I'm sure she's enjoying herself no longer encumbered by her body. In fact, wherever Grandma is, I'm sure she's smiling.

The Sounds of Silence

My younger son recently said to me, "The reason you talk so much, Mom, is that you never had to listen as a child. Grandma and Grandpa didn't talk, so you didn't have to listen!"

When deaf people "talk" to each other it's so fast, so animated, expressive and non-stop. One has to practically jump on the other person to get a word in.

My folks "talked" to me all the time—double time, with signs and voice. Fortunately they had good voice control, especially Mom, and Dad was always using his voice as he was forever the socialite, talking with all the neighbors and showing magic tricks to kids everywhere. Silence is not always golden. My parents were far from silent.

It is true that as an adult I relish quiet. Many friends tell me when they get up in the morning they immediately turn on the radio or TV. When I am home alone I rarely play the radio or watch TV during the day. I prefer going out with one couple rather than a crowd. I've been told I have peripheral *hearing* so I unintentionally catch what other people are saying. Now all this may indeed be a result of either growing up as an only child or having deaf parents.

My folks kept a dictionary handy and were always making lists of new words and asking pronunciations. They both had a keen thirst for knowledge. They were always cutting out sayings and poems. Dad took exceptional pride in his job at the newspaper as a proofreader and always said he was not just a typesetter or the fancy word *linotype operator*. He probably thought that the printing of the paper was his sole responsibility. He may have been right.

Sorry son, but I sure did listen as a child. Listened with my eyes and ears. Maybe I talk so much now because one sense of my speech pattern is missing. After all, I now only talk with my voice. Gee, how much more meaningful and expressive talking is with both voice and sign!

CHAPTER 7

Conclusions

Commentary

I read recently that someone thought TV was not made for deaf people. I have to completely disagree. My father was in seventh heaven when we finally got our set. Since he was an avid sports fan he was in his glory. After his retirement, the world was his. He never had a dull moment. I really believed TV prolonged his life.

For my mother, closed captioning was a boon. The world was brought so much closer to her. Foreign films have a large audience in the deaf world, for obvious reasons. Mom could watch the same programs as I and we could share the laughter or tears.

Thanks to Senator Tom Harkin, all television sets thirteen inches and larger since July 1, 1993, are required to have built in caption decoders. Money for a decoder will no longer have to be a factor on whether or not a family should purchase one.

Now deaf and hearing people can rehash the soaps the next day, together. Just think of what you talk about on arriving to work first thing in the morning. It's a simple common everyday occurrence that helps bring people closer.

Memories

I grew up in an extremely privileged environment. My parents gave me unconditional love and nurtured me through my childhood, teens and on to adulthood. Mom was the disciplinarian and Daddy, thinking I could do no wrong, was constantly spoiling me and undoing all of Mom's rules.

I have already told you of my two aunts. In addition, Mom saw to it that I had ballet lessons, tap lessons and loving every kind of dance, Mom, Bertye, Ida and I all went together whenever we went to a ballet or any show with dancing. I took Mom with me to the Metropolitan Opera at Lincoln Center and she enjoyed the sheer grandeur of it. She would ask me, what it was all about being in a foreign language. Well, half the time I didn't know either.

Yes, there were times I would correct Mom's speech and maybe not. She would pronounce Bravo with a long A. Somehow that would make it sound unique. So I let it go for a while enjoying it. Eventually I told her and she laughed and continued saying it. So there!

Dad saw to it that I knew every sport there was. Every year we would go to Randall's Island for the track meets. I have already mentioned our regular baseball games. He introduced me to basketball, and even had me meet some of the all-time greats. In my teens, hockey was a big event in our neighborhood and I would go with my friends to Madison Square garden every New Years' Eve. Mom, Dad and I would run and run at picnics, beaches, wherever. We were all good runners, the three of us, and good at throwing and catching. Life was never dull.

All of this may sound very protective, but at the proper time, they gave me free reign and cut the cord.

Their circle was so vast, and now that they are gone I wonder, "When will I ever use sign again? With whom shall I practice?"

I have returned to Mom's last residence several times, perhaps to hold on to the past, perhaps to hold on to my childhood, or just not ready to let go. The loss seems so intense. It seems inconceivable for me to have only one world—a world without sign and deaf people. They were so much a part of my life. One thing I do know; if something should happen to me and I couldn't speak, I bet I'll be able to finger spell as my mother did right to the end.

The times with my parents play on in my memory now, as brightly as when my sons alight from the plane bringing them home from California.

My parents are now physically gone, but I am still here and so are my children. Hopefully, all the values, attributes and positive outlook of my parents have been passed on to us. If we have attained some degree of accomplishment in our lives and achieved a sense of morality, we indeed owe it to them.

Our children are, after all, the sum of us. I like to think that the apple really does not fall far from the tree!

This writing has been a wonderful catharsis and excellent therapy. It is my hope that if I am lucky enough to have others read this, they may benefit from the knowledge that being hearing with deaf parents, or deaf with hearing parents, or all deaf, need not be a burden, but rather "THE BEST OF ALL POSSIBLE WORLDS."

Recipes

Miriam's Spaghetti Croquettes

Left over spaghetti with sauce-(chopped up)

Matzoh Meal

One egg

Mix all together-shape into patties

Pan fry in something terribly unhealthful (like Mazola oil)

Brown and turn over

   Delicious!!!

   Chocolate Cream Pie

My T Fine Chocolate pudding (it has to be My-T-Fine)

Graham crackers

Whipped cream (the real stuff, no aerosol cans back then)

Cook pudding with milk (yes real milk) until nice and smooth

Grate crackers

Put cracker mix in bottom of Pyrex dish-pour smooth pudding into dish

Make real whipped cream and spoon on top

   Ummmm!!!

Notes

H.A.D.—Hebrew Association of the Deaf

TTY or TDD (phone for the hearing impaired)
        Teletypewriter
        Telecommunications device for the deaf

THE CROWD—five couples that remained friends forever

Mom's sayings:

    SO THERE!!

    I read an article!

    If you don't mind my saying so?

    That's that!

    Some nerve!

    FANCY!

About the Author

Lila Worzel Miller, a graduate of Brooklyn College
Is a retired teacher from the New York City Board of
Education. Her last ten years of teaching was in Special
Education with autistic children.
She lives in New City, N.Y. and Delray Beach, Florida with
her husband, George. Their sons and daughter-in law live
in California.